THE MINDFUL PRESCHOOLER

GEORGE BONNER
&
SAMANTHA MILLIGAN
ILLUSTRATED BY
KENDYL KAUTERMAN

The Mindful Preschooler

Published by Gatekeeper Press
2167 Stringtown Rd, Suite 109
Columbus, OH 43123-2989
www.GatekeeperPress.com

Illustrations by Kendyl Kauterman
Editing by Colin Brady

Library of Congress Control Number: 2020939665

ISBN (paperback): 9781662901324
eISBN: 9781662901331

Reviews

I absolutely love the book. It is exactly what the world needs right now. I have never seen a book like this before. It is beautifully written from beginning to end and it has wonderful ways to remind children to stay mindful, relaxed and healthy. To find a book that teaches a child how to meditate is amazing! I am a mother of a little boy who has experienced severe trauma, the book is truly helpful and will be a part of our bedtime routine.

We highly recommend this book to anyone with a family that is trying to learn about and practice healthy living!

Susan Morris
President of the Haley Morris Foundation

I absolutely loved The Mindful Preschooler! It shares all the happy components to a young learner's day with such positive dialogue. It truly describes the perfect preschool experience and would get any child excited for school and friends! I will definitely read this to my four-year-old so he knows how wonderful school, teachers and friends can be! Beautifully written!

Kristy Cichonski
Special Education Teacher

Preschoolers are naturally "mindful"—living in the present moment. However, as they confront new challenges, strong emotions lead to dysregulation and confusion. At last, a book is here to show them what to expect as they prepare for school. This beautiful, appropriately paced descriptive story takes children through a "day in the life." It culminates in a breathing technique that all children can take with them and use for those inevitable moments when things do not go their way and strong emotions surface. Thank you, Samantha, George, and Kendyl for bringing us this delightful and wise book. Parents should read it to their children the night before they go off to school and then over and over again.

Eric D. Berger, MD
General and Developmental Pediatrician
Center City Pediatrics

In Loving Memory of

Mary Jane Hones

"Gram"

1923-2018

Gram, thank you for being the inspiration for The Mindful
Preschooler. I got into mediation after you passed away and it has
open my mind on how I see things in the world. I was very lucky to
have you as my great-grandmother and that I got to lived next door
to you for twenty-three years. My favorite memories of you were
dancing in your house and drying dishes after dinner on a Sunday.
You gave me the best childhood and life lessons that I will cherish
for the rest of my life. I love you, forever and always.

Love,

Samantha

To Anna, my eternal princess.

Love,

Uncle George

Mom says, "Good Morning Anna. It's time to get up for school." Anna says, "Mommy, I do not want to go to school. I want to stay with you and Daddy and eat ice cream all day." Mom says, "Today is a special day, you are going to make new friends and learn some new things."

Mom says, "Anna, time to brush your teeth with your princess toothbrush. When you're brushing your teeth, pay close attention when brushing your teeth." Anna says, "Yes Mommy, I love how my teeth feel clean and look shiny after I brush them."

Anna gets dropped off at school and says good morning to her class and teachers, Ms. Sam and Ms. Vanessa. She waves and smiles at her classmates and Ms. Sam and Ms. Vanessa. Anna's friends say good morning to Anna.

Anna and her friend Bailey are playing together. They noticed another student is by themselves. Anna says, "Do you want to play with us and be our friend?" Brayden says, "Yes, I would like to play and be your friend". Ms. Sam watches her students and smiles at a new friendship blossoming in the classroom. The kids continue to play together.

Ms. Sam says "Five minutes until clean up, remember to pay attention when putting toys away and to help each other out. Everyone must work as a team." The class replies in agreement, "Yes Ms. Sam."

Anna and her friends sit at the circle time rug and listen to Ms. Sam speak. Ms. Sam says "Good Morning class, we need to listen today and pay attention. We are going to make a healthy snack and I need your helping hands, listening ears, and everyone working together." Anna and her classmates agree to Ms. Sam's directions.

Ms. Sam gives directions to Anna and classmates to line up and wash hands before touching food. Ms. Sam says, "Remember to wash your hands on both sides and in between your fingers, sing your ABCs, and dry your hands completely." Anna and classmates happily agree to wash their hands and line up to do the next task.

Ms. Sam, Ms. Vanessa, Anna, and the classmates sit at a round table with fruit, cups, spoons, and bowls. Ms. Sam says, "We are all going to work together and create a healthy snack with our favorite fruit. As the bowl comes around, everyone will pour their favorite fruit in the bowl. Once we are done stirring the fruit, everyone will put the fruit in their bowl and pass to their neighbor and reply, 'thank you'"!

Ms. Vanessa asks her students, "What are some of your favorite fruits?" Molly says "orange." Nolan says "apple." Bella says "blueberries." Colin says "mango." Ms. Vanessa smiles at the responses from her students and says, "those are wonderful answers."

Anna passes the bowl to Charlie. Charlie says, "but I want ice cream." Ms. Vanessa tells Charlie ice cream is okay to have but it is not a healthy snack. Charlie says "Okay, I will have the fruit salad, please."

Anna and her classmates get up from nap time, clean up, and line up for the bathroom. Ms. Sam says, "Good afternoon students, I hope you had a nice nap. We have a busy afternoon." Anna says, "What are we doing this afternoon?" Ms. Sam says, "We are going to draw our favorite animal with our favorite color." Anna says, "Yea!". Lucas says, "My favorite animal is a tiger. I am going to paint it orange." Adrianna says, "My favorite animal is a butterfly. I am going to paint it purple." Ms. Sam is very happy that her students are excited about the art project this afternoon.

Ms. Sam, Anna, Lucas, and Adrianna sit around the table with art supply: color paint, papers, t-shirts and paint brushes. Ms. Sam says "Anna, Lucas, and Adrianna, please put on your t-shirt before the art project."

Anna says, "Why do we have to put a t-shirt on for our art project?" Ms. Sam says, "Anna, you need to put a t-shirt on so your clothes don't get messy. Mommy and Daddy work very hard so Anna has nice clothes to wear to school." Anna says, "Thank you Ms. Sam, I understand." Anna, Lucas, and Adrianna put their t-shirts on and are ready to work on their art project. Ms. Sam says "Remember students, be creative and use bold and bright colors. This is your masterpiece."

After working on the art project, Ms. Sam calls Anna and the class to form a circle on the rug. Ms. Sam says, "Everyone sit in a circle and close your eyes. Please follow my instructions. Place both of your hands on your belly. Next, slowly breathe in and out through your nose. As you breathe in, your belly expands and gets bigger. As you breathe out through your nose, your belly gets smaller. Repeat this exercise ten times. Now as you breathe in, imagine two red balloons inside your chest. As you breathe in the red balloons get bigger. As you breathe out the red balloons become smaller. Continue this exercise ten times with your eyes closed. Anna and the class practice this exercise with Ms. Sam and Ms. Vanessa. Ms. Sam says, "Think of happy thoughts while paying attention to your breathing slowly through your nose."

After the meditation, Ms. Sam, Ms. Vanessa, Anna, and the class open their eyes slowly. Ms. Sam says, "How is everyone feeling after doing the breathing exercise?" Anna says, "I feel happy." Mia says, "I feel relaxed." Matthew says, "I feel calm." Ben says, "I feel silly." The class starts to laugh and giggle together. Ms. Sam and Ms. Vanessa smile as they appreciate the different personalities of students.

Ms. Sam and Ms. Vanessa say, "To be mindful is to pay attention in the present moment without distractions." Ms. Vanessa asks, "As we come to the end of the school day, what was your favorite part of the day?" Anna says, "The fruit salad and I made a new friend." Lucas says, "The art project." Nicholas says, "Playing with the toys." Anna and her classmates are very happy sharing their thoughts. It makes them feel special that Ms. Sam and Ms. Vanessa include them in the class discussion.

Anna and Margot are playing dress up. As they are playing dress up, Anna's mom walks into the classroom. Mom says, "Anna, I miss you so much. How was your day?" Anna says, "Mom, I miss you too. My day was wonderful." Mom says, "Anna, say goodbye to Margot, your class, Ms. Sam, and Ms. Vanessa. Tell them you will see them tomorrow. Anna says, "Okay Mommy. Goodbye Margot, friends, Ms. Sam, and Ms. Vanessa." Margot says, "Goodbye Anna." Anna gets her backpack and her lunch box with her mom. They leave to go home for dinner.

Anna, Mom, and Dad are at the dinner table to talk about their day. Mom says, "How was your day Kevin?" Dad says, "My day was great. How was your day Elizabeth?" Mom says, "My day was wonderful. How was your day Anna?" Anna says, "My day was a special day. I learned that every moment can be special when I pay attention and live in the moment." Mom and Dad say, "That is amazing Anna. We love you so much." Anna says, "I love you too Mommy and Daddy."

Anna's mom says to her, "Let's go down to Somerset Splits and get your favorite ice cream." Anna responds with a smile on her face, "Yes Mommy, I would like Cookies and Cream because that is Ms. Vanessa's favorite ice cream flavor."

CPSIA information can be obtained
at www.ICGtesting.com
Printed in the USA
BVHW092005080920
588352BV00006B/264